Sign Language

An exhibition of *Sign Language* is organized by the Amon Carter Museum, Fort
Worth, Texas. Current exhibition schedule: Burden Gallery, New York, New York,
March 16–April 22, 1989. Amon Carter Museum, Fort Worth, Texas,
July 22–September 10, 1989.

Aperture Foundation gratefully acknowledges the support of Lemuel C. and Martha
Joe Hawes Hutchins, the Vaughn Foundation, and Half Price Books, Records,
and Magazines, Inc. in making this publication possible.

Composition by David E. Seham Associates, Inc., Metuchen, New Jersey.
Printed and bound in Hong Kong by Everbest Printing Co., Ltd.
Color separations by Rainbow Graphic Arts Co., Ltd.

ISBN 0-89381-333-8

for Mom and Dad

Tse Bii'Nidzisgai

Monument Valley's Navajo name is *Tse Bii'Nidzisgai* (White Rocks Inside). The story is that the valley is where "Rocks Are Pointing Upward" (*Tsenideezhazhaii*). Before that it was called White Rocks Inside. As they tell the story there used to be monsters out there. The monsters were the enemies of the Navajo and used to be somewhere in White Rocks Inside.

There are Holy People who live there now and they say that important Holy Way ceremonial stories were originally formed there. The valley is protected.

They also say that flying Eagle People by the name of "Sky Travelers" used these Rocks Pointing Upward to aid their travel. These Eagle People used to park on Rocks Pointing Upward. From there they used to watch for things to eat. From the Rocks Pointing Upward they also used to pray for the Black Rain (hard and fast with thunder and lightning, also called Male Rain) that is there.

The Rocks Pointing Upward that are red are different. The Red Rocks Pointing Upward represent the enemy, the different dangers, the things that are not good. They say that is the reason they were made. So no one should ever be there or go near there at all.

Now, for some, the valley's purpose is sightseeing. For others its purpose is to produce good minds and good thoughts, and hogans are built here and there. People feel proud and have good thoughts, even if they have never seen Rocks Pointing Upward. When they think of the place, they have good thoughts.

This is all I will talk about concerning White Rocks Inside as it is all I have been told.

—MIKE MITCHELL

Navajo window washer, Monument Valley Tribal Park, Arizona, 1984

Markings on Highway 380 near Carrizozo, New Mexico, 1986

Sign Language

CONTEMPORARY SOUTHWEST NATIVE AMERICA

PHOTOGRAPHS BY SKEET McAULEY

INTRODUCTION BY N. SCOTT MOMADAY
The Way It Is BY LUCI TAPAHONSO
TRADITIONAL NAVAJO STORIES BY MIKE MITCHELL
"As the Mementoes of the Race" BY MARTHA A. SANDWEISS

APERTURE

A NEW IMAGES BOOK

Naatsis'aan

THIS PICTURE is from on top of *Dzilijiin* (Black Mountain) and way over there is Navajo Mountain or *Naatsis'aan*. The mountain contains holy songs. There are roads and clouds too. There is also sunshine on Mother Earth.

When you look at a place, you look around. What do you notice? What do you understand of what you see? What different things do you see? How will you understand what is there?

They say that the Mother Earth intends for us to make life's plans with love.

When you look way over there it seems like it looks back at you. With this in mind, you make plans knowing the earth is looking back at you. You wonder why it's that way, you think about it, and you have a certain pattern which will affect your plans for making a living.

In this place there are roads, plants, Mother Earth, and the mountain that appears there, Navajo Mountain. Then clouds, and sunshine, all of which affect your frame of mind in thinking about your plans. They say your plans of living and acting are to be respectful of these. It is not only that it is beautiful way out there, nor only that it is very good; that is not the point. The point is this is a very holy place. So they say that there is sunshine, there is wind, and together they form the place. There are plants, trees, rocks, and mountains put there with clouds roaming around. The sunrays shine on them with the wind and air participating.

When you look way out towards the horizon, you wonder how and when it was made that way. You wonder who made it, for what purpose, and you will think about plans you will make from it. Your plans will form from thinking and really concentrating on what you are looking at out there.

Then, somehow, you look and something does not appear just right, maybe not too bad, and you look way out towards the horizon. Before you know it your mind is whole again. Even though you might think nothing of it, you are whole again. Maybe you might not be feeling good, with aches all over your body, pains on the knees, you feel cranky. Then you will be feeling fine again and all kinds of negative thoughts will be removed.

The old people's stories from way back, with the holy prayers and holy songs, have set the plan.

So the songs, the winds, the sunshine, Mother Earth, mountains, plants, and everything else seem to walk together. It seems like they all talk, and it seems like they will talk to you when you just look out and see trees, rocks, mountains, and clouds roaming by with rain coming down. And you look out among all that, compare your thoughts with all that, and happily you will get healed again in a beautiful way. That is why the place is there and in your thoughts. So this is the way it is when you look out towards the horizons.

Then there is the story behind all this. They say that Mother Earth has a perfect plan in store for everything: the mountains, dark clouds, whatever the universe has in store, the sunshine which shines on the planet Mother Earth, the way it is with the wind and air, the roads, the rocks, and everything. All kinds of plants and animals, starting from the smallest kinds of bugs you see, live there. They say that they are there with minds and plans of their own. That is the way the old people's stories go.

Then there are the plants which are really different from one another, each with different odors when you smell them. When you smell them, you breathe their odors in through your whole body system, through the blood veins, and it makes you feel good. Some of these things you don't notice, but they really exist that way. Way out there you can see *Naatsis'aan,* and that's the way the story goes about it.

There are many more stories about *Naatsis'aan,* but I will tell only this much about the mountain.   —M. M.

Overlooking coal conveyer toward Navajo Mountain from Black Mesa, Arizona, 1985

Offering at Apache Sunrise Ceremony, White River, Arizona, 1985

Introduction

BY N. SCOTT MOMADAY

THE AMERICAN SOUTHWEST is a landscape of great power and beauty. And it is sacred. The native inhabitants of that landscape are a people of great spiritual reserves. Their relationship to the land is ancient: It is predicated, not upon occupation or possession, much less upon title and deed and treaty; rather it is predicated upon belief, a profound belief in the earth as sacred ground.

> May it be delightful my house;
> From my head may it be delightful;
> To my feet may it be delightful;
> Where I lie may it be delightful;
> All above me may it be delightful;
> All around me may it be delightful.

This house-blessing from the Navajo is very nearly a definition of man's relation to the world around him. The singer stands at the center of being. He acknowledges in the language of prayer the equation of body, mind, and spirit as their life extends outward to infinity. It is a formula which affirms man's existence in the universe.

Sign Language is about the land, and Skeet McAuley's photographs clearly remark this element of the sacred, but they speak to something else as well.

The photograph, "Apache Mother and Child, White River, Arizona, 1985" (page 39), seems a classic evocation of the traditional Native-American world. At first glance we might well take this to be a nineteenth-century scene. The setting is rustic, if not wild. The long blue mesa in the distance is unmistakably "Indian Country," as it has existed for untold time. The woman's dress is the real thing; irrefutably Apache, homemade, beautiful and distinctive. And the woman herself is Apache; handsome and strong. She is straight, and her facial features bespeak a seriousness and integrity that are peculiarly indigenous. It is a photograph of conspicuous character and authenticity. The composition is whole, the symmetry precise, the perspective true. But there are anachronisms, there are ironies about, very subtle juxtapositions that return our awareness upon the contemporary world. Anachronism is one of McAuley's subjects. A child in the shadowy left foreground is romping. Far from traditional, his dress is so modern as to constitute a caricature. He might be modeling an outfit from the children's department at Saks. And on the same level, at the right, are a scattering of bright aluminum cans. We take notice of these details, but not at once.

They proceed, almost subliminally, upon our awareness. They somehow exceed our expectations; at last they take us by surprise. But they ring true. We understand that we are observing not what was, as in a photograph by Edward S. Curtis, for example, but what is.

McAuley is not a Native American (do not lose the force of the capitals here), but his view of the Native American world is entirely valid. I suspect that he sees that world in the 1980s with as much, if not more, clarity than do most of us, even those of us who are especially concerned to understand that world. His photographs are revelations.

whose life is this?
whose life is this?

the one who stole
played interstate romance on I-40
  (on summer nights, it's easy, she said later)

she was caught on the trail
of a lone navajo bachelor in a low 280-zx
  on that undulating stretch from gallup to albuquerque

the one who stole
could say it was those hills, those sheer red cliffs
  that heavy full moon or the night brimming with wildflower scent

  all those elements conspired, she said,
  causing the chase down I-40, it wasn't really me, she said.

This poem, "Whose Life Is This," by the gifted Navajo poet, Luci Tapahonso, reflects in words what McAuley reflects in photographic images. There again the sacred earth, redefined in some way by the imposition of the modern, the contemporary. What we get, more often than not, and what is all that we can ask, are the enigmatic realities, the mysteries which give us to wonder and be glad. Perhaps dichotomy here is the principal reality. And perhaps dichotomy, rather than resolution, is what we ought to acknowledge and appreciate. McAuley seems to say so.

Mike Mitchell's texts are really stories, quintessential realizations of the landscape in words, and the stories are peculiarly native in character. They constitute a verbal dimension which complements the visual easily and fortunately. The collaboration is what it ought to be, a book that is worth looking into for its own sake.

It is not my purpose here to address Skeet McAuley's photographs individually, but I cannot help commenting upon "Navajo Window Washer, Monument Valley, Arizona, 1984." It seems to concentrate the purpose and accomplishment of McAuley's artistry. Consider: the monoliths float away in some unspeakable dimension of space and distance and time. Each of them is framed like pieces in a gallery by new and man-made geometries. The window washer, a man whose roots reach down into this landscape through many generations, regards us through plate glass and eyeglasses. He wears, with the possible exception of the beaded belt, what any student at any American university of the 1980s might wear. Here are riddles of time. Looking at this truly remarkable photography, it is somewhat difficult to say what kind of fix we have on time. There is the window washer, a young man of the moment, emphatically moored to our own time. There is the sign that directs our attention to a dinosaur track millions of years old. And there are the great monoliths in the distance, which stand beyond time.

Here are images which are clear and respectful, playful and grave, profound and mysterious. They are a concentration of the American earth, its surface and its depth.

The Way It Is

BY LUCI TAPAHONSO

aMERICAN INDIANS have been portrayed since the 1600s in one of two ways: the "noble savage" and the "red devil." The noble savage is brave, stoic, attired in traditional regalia and purporting an unspeakable mystique. The red devil is the drunk, the amoral tomahawk wielder. There has been no middle ground between these two extremes in literature and the media.

Until recently, this issue of the Indian image has not been addressed. Skeet McAuley's photographs confront this dilemma head-on. His portrayal of contemporary Indians in the Southwest can be seen as unusual, awkward, and perhaps contradictory to what the Anglos in the U.S. have been taught about Indians. Yet non-Indians depicted in these same photographs in similar situations would most likely be considered the norm and readily accepted.

Because such images are imprinted in the American psyche, Indians are not considered part of this country's mainstream. Major polls and demographic surveys rarely include "American Indians" as a meaningful segment of America; instead we fall into the category labeled "other" or "unknown." This fact is not overlooked by us, the Indian people. We are aware of this oversight by the media and the other symbolic "reflectors" of our society.

The effect of this oversight on the Indian child can scarcely be de-termined. Generations of Indian people have grown up seeing light-skinned, fair-haired people portrayed on billboards, in commercials, and in educational texts as the "true" Americans. The American media has ignored the Indian identity and the Indian "self" has not been reinforced. Advertising does not portray Indians as "real people" who enjoy red meat or drive particular automobiles symbolizing "the heartbeat of America"; it is interesting to surmise how the whole of the United States, including Indians, would perceive minorities if it did.

It is rare and, indeed, very exciting to see an Indian person in a commercial advertisement. Word travels fast when that happens. Nunzio's Pizza in Albuquerque, New Mexico, ran commercials featuring Jose Rey Toledo of Jemez Pueblo talking about his "native land—Italy" while wearing typical Pueblo attire—jewelry, moccasins, and hair tied in a chongo. Because of the ironic humor, because Indian grandfathers specialize in playing tricks and jokes on their grandchildren, and because Jose Rey Toledo is a respected and well-known elder in the Indian communities, word of this commercial spread fast among Indians in New Mexico. It was the cause of recognition and celebration of sorts on the reservations and in the pueblos. His portrayal was not in the categories which the media usually associates with Indians but as a typical sight in the Southwest. It showed Indians as we live today—enjoying pizza as one of our favorite foods, including humor and fun as part of our daily lives, and recognizing the importance of preserving traditional knowledge.

Similarly, Skeet McAuley's photographs show the complexities of our lives today. The moments he captures are rare and insightful glimpses into typical reservation life, and show the integration of modern American lifestyles and the old ritual ways of our ancestors. Indian life in this country is not simple and straightforward, and contrary to the usual portrayals of the Indian as being "caught between two worlds," McAuley's photographs show an accepted merging of the two cultures and an unspoken appreciation of American technology. Thus, although American society overlooks the Indian peoples, Indians accept and live with what America has to offer. These photographs show Indian people appreciating and embracing American ways more than non-Indian citizens usually understand.

Perhaps then the "plight of the Indian" is not how the Indian assimilates or "fits" into America but how America accepts Indians as "regular" Americans. These images may be disturbing because they conflict with images people have of how Indians are "supposed" to look or live. Yet Indians view these photographs as an acknowledgement and statement long overdue because it's rare that their everyday circumstances are featured in widely distributed publications such as this book.

Before the arrival of the Europeans, traditional lifestyles were fairly difficult and depended on the elements and knowledge associated with the land, ceremonies, and the universe. Arising from this knowledge is the basic philosophy still adhered to today. One must do the best one can with the way things are—as the Navajo phrase, *Taa hooajii twiitaaya,* conveys. This philosophy encompasses the total environment: the weather, the land, and the individual, and ensures that all tasks associated with the economic well-being of the family are shared by all able family members. Whether these tasks are working in the fields or building a home, it is the same today: making and painting pottery, running a frybread stand at the fairs, or selling jewelry off the interstate highway.

The photograph of the roadside vendors portrays a way of life for many Indian families (page 62). Virtually all families on the reservations have sold various items to earn money at one time or another—jewelry,

food, pottery, rugs, or crops from the fall harvest. Such experience is so common, it makes up a wealth of stories, jokes, and memories. The appearance of these makeshift stores can be misleading to the visitor. The structure itself is basic—a shelter from the hot sun, which contains a counter and usually a table to eat from and a chair or two. The floor is bare and, in the middle of the desert, the shaded dirt is cool compared to the hot sand outside. Vendors usually pack their lunches in the morning and stay the entire day. Lunch and drinks are generally stored under the counter and water is kept in a cooler or a five-gallon jerry can in the corner. Appearances suggest that life is hard and making ends meet on the reservation is a matter of quiet desperation, of long days in the sun, and crying children underfoot everyday.

Not apparent in this visual image is the atmosphere surrounding these "new" traditions—the time and care that goes into the preparation of things to pack, the stories and news one hears at the stand, the children exploring and playing in the dirt with toys, and the quiet moments in between customers to sing, tell stories, and go for walks looking for whatever plants might be in season. Selling to the tourists can also lead to a treasury of stories and cherished memories.

For instance, once as we were driving to Gallup, New Mexico, on Interstate 40 near Grants, a friend from Acoma Pueblo told this story:

See those rocks up there? (pointing to a steep craggy hillside.) That's where we buried the potteries every evening after we got through selling. We didn't have a car and they were too heavy for Mama or any of us to carry home each evening. There's a crevice wide enough up there—we wrapped the potteries in a soft blanket and my brother and I, each carrying one end, climbed up there carefully and placed it inside. Mama would be watching us and saying, "Be careful, boys, watch your step." Other people also kept their potteries up there in their own places that they had. In the morning, you would see them carrying their bundles of pottery slowly and carefully off the hill. I remember we walked home slowly with my mother and sometimes she sang or told us stories about places or plants we saw on the way. We had a particular path we took each morning and evening. It's all grown over now but we mention it sometimes as we drive by and say, "Remember when we used to sell, Mama, we used that path?" I remember that.

Such stories become vividly connected with the land surrounding the stands. Much more than an economic necessity, the stands then become of a new ritual, a new tradition.

Stories of those times and places will be told by the children years from now or this evening at home about the tourist from Michigan who wanted to know the "deep" meaning behind a design the silversmith simply liked. She made up a harmless little story about it just then because the tourist wanted one to tell people back home when they admired his bolo tie. He would have been disappointed otherwise. Every seller or vendor has a number of such stories. Indeed, what seems a desperate situation to outsiders provides a treasury of memories and stories far removed from the monetary aspects of life.

Necessary elements of daily life such as portable toilets are usually nearby wherever these stands are located. At Laguna, west of the toilets are several wooden stands selling that wonderful Pueblo ovenbread, tamales spiced just right, and of course, silver and turquoise jewelry. Tourists stop to use the bathroom, buy jewelry, and take pictures of the historic marker and the pueblo. Indian people stop to buy tamales and bread to eat on the way home, use the bathroom, find out when the next feast days are, and try again to locate the friend one went to Indian school with years ago.

The influence of technology has had its impact on Indian country as much as anywhere else. When people sell off the highway with no electricity or running water nearby, then the use of an ice chest is a wonderful advantage. To be able to drink ice water on a hot summer day in the middle of the desert still boggles some Indian minds. I relive the long afternoons of my childhood when my sister and I see an ice chest filled with ice cubes. We laugh and say, "Remember? She didn't share." A cousin brought an ice chest filled with ice and water jars to the fields where we sometimes worked. We had our water in the shade under some shrubs and, while it was cool, it was not cold like the ice water she was drinking. "Where did you get the ice?" we asked hopefully, thinking she would offer us some. "At home," she said, drinking ice water. She didn't offer us any and we would not ask. So we watched her, envious of the ice-filled cooler and sweating water jars.

Memories of working in the cucumber fields long ago inspired the following poem:

INDEPENDENCE

I guess I've always savored
independence in my own way.
When I was 9, I received my first paycheck
80¢ for picking cucumbers in the large fields
northwest of Shiprock on the mesas.
I cashed it and right away bought myself
a dreamsicle ice cream and popsicles
for my sisters after Sunday school.
We walked home slowly—3 miles from
Chief Grocery on a July afternoon.

It was sure good to be independent,
I thought, savoring a melting dreamsicle.

The carnival depicted in McAuley's photographs is another new tradition for many Indian people. The carnival only comes to the reservation two or three times a year—sometimes less depending on where one lives. Going to the carnival means driving miles and preparing to spend a night or the whole day in the vicinity. Usually a carnival is contracted in conjunction with a fair. In the pueblos, it's during a feast day that a carnival arrives. In some ways, it seems inconsistent that a symbol of American tawdriness and frivolity would be so well-attended in Indian country.

Dr. Rina Swentzell of Santa Clara Pueblo took a university class in Southwest studies to Cochiti Pueblo on one of the feast days. The non-Indian students expressed dismay at the fact that a few hundred yards away from the village plaza where ritual dances were being held, carnies were hawking various games and prizes in loud, boisterous voices. They didn't understand why the carnival was allowed there. Dr. Swentzell smiled and related the following story:

When I was a child, feast days were so exciting. If I was taking part, we began practicing weeks in advance. Every morning and evening was spent practicing. We were anxious for the day to arrive not only for the dances, the many visitors, the fun of meeting other kids but also the carnival! I loved the rides! When my group was through dancing, sometimes I didn't even change my dance outfit. I just ran over and got in line for the ferris wheel. I enjoyed it so much. At night, I fell asleep exhausted from dancing, the rides and walking around and around at the carnival.

The students slowly came to the realization that Indian children enjoy the very same things as their non-Indian peers. Again the old stereotype of the Indian as stoic, serious, and menacingly quiet has pervaded American culture in subtle ways.

Similarly, the experience of riding a ferris wheel in the middle of the desert near Kayenta is unlike any other. Memories of Indian children's trips to the carnival will be forever intermingled with the desert night air and the huge monoliths looming silent in the desert. Riding the sky glider or the giant ferris wheel at the Arizona State Fair or in Albuquerque lacks so much in comparison.

In a related way, video games, video cameras and various electronic gadgets have found their way into Navajoland. For generations, the Navajo people have depended on the use of memory, telling stories, and listening to pass along values, history, and language. As Navajo children enter schools and parents leave the reservation for jobs or education, the old way of learning is disrupted. Contemporary technology becomes beneficial in a different and powerful way. A social event can be taped on video and shared with relatives in distant cities who cannot attend. Several Navajo students who attend college off the reservation record family meals and get-togethers to listen to when they are away. The voices of family and exchange of stories, food and jokes can be far more encouraging than a session with a college advisor. For those tribal members who must be away, technology is a positive tool against isolation and a welcome aspect of living in America.

In addition, Navajo people who work with large machinery and powerful tools of industry approach their work with a serious intensity. This type of work demands a combination of awe, respect, and fear. The power of the individual in this situation is at once overwhelming and at the same time meaningless should something go awry. In this situation, respect is forced. The employee will leave at a specified time and then it is over. His allegiance and attention to the matter is measured only by hours and a paycheck. This is a common way of earning a living for many Americans.

But the Indian way of ensuring a good life and of ensuring the means of earning a good living is very different and is still adhered to today. Sweatbaths and ceremonies are part of these ancient life-enhancing rituals. Many of the ceremonies include offering to the people in attendance, the relatives who help, and are given to commemorate a good harvest. Such gatherings are ceremonial, religious, social, and at times, political. A time for the community and family members to congregate. All have a responsibility at these gatherings, whether it is to bring "throw" things, donate livestock, help cook, or bring firewood. Perhaps in traditional times, the items shown in the photograph at Apache would have been bundles of herbs, ears of corn, precious stones, rugs, and small melons (page 10). Today, American products are used as they are readily available and relatively inexpensive. One need only unwrap a package of Cracker Jacks or breakfast cereals and begin distributing. In a culture where the majority of the people (both male and female) work five or six days a weeks, gathering herbs and tying ears of corn is much too time-consuming compared to going to the supermarket and buying products in quantity.

The monetary aspects of the ritual can be significant. Yet the symbolic meaning overshadows the expense; "give-aways," "throws," and "grab days" are expressions of gratitude by the family that hosts the activity. While the events that call for such a sharing vary from tribe to tribe, the basic ideas of generosity and gratitude prevail. In this sharing, all people attending—observers and participants, Indian and non-Indian— become a part of the ritual. The people attending receive explicit instructions on how they are, in part, responsible for the effectiveness of the ceremony and what those responsibilities are. In this sense, the effects are longlasting and concern not only the people and the land but also the total environment.

Other photographs by McAuley show that young people throughout America, including Navajo youths, fall victim to fads, current trends, and popular music. At cultural events, one is bound to see teen-agers with black tee-shirts promoting a particular band or type of music. Indian adults, for the most part, accept it as a passing interest; young Indian people know not to go to sacred places with radios, tape players, or loud motorcycles. Still, while the influence of contemporary America is in strong evidence on the reservations, the influence of Navajo or Indian philosophy is less visible. What the young girl selling cotton candy at the Window Rock fair knows about Navajo history or tradition is lost in a photograph (page 46).

The young boy is riding his motorbike beneath Window Rock, outside the headquarters of the Navajo Chairman's office (page 49). The sacred properties of Window Rock and traditional stories connected with it overlook the center of modern Navajo politics and the paradoxes that can surround a democratic system of government. This boy is in the center of two contrasting symbols of Navajo life today. Fifty years ago, this young boy may have been posing on a fine sorrel horse but like countless other American boys, today he poses with pride on his motorbike, in front of an ancient sacred place. There is a sense of ease and comfort in his posture, he is welcome in either place as a Navajo child. The implication is that he is able to play outside the Chairman's office or pay his respects at Window Rock. In contrast, the president of this country is considered far too vulnerable to allow children to play near the White House.

As bicycles are the transportation of choice for young people, pickup trucks are also a very common adult choice on the reservations. There are jokes about "not being Indian if one doesn't drive a pickup." Standard family cars are considered too fragile for reservation dirt roads and not suitable for hauling cargo of any type. It is said that whenever Indians get together, there is bound to be a circle of pickup trucks surrounding the location. In the photographs in *Sign Language,* pickup trucks appear in the majority of them, making it evident that Indians are changing. Yet this change is still tied to the land, the terrain, and the beliefs of the family. Many families have their vehicles "blessed" by a medicine-person upon purchase to protect themselves and their pickups. This con-

nection is also apparent in the naming of car parts in Navajo—the car's battery is called *bijei* meaning the "heart." The headlights are called *binaa*—the "eyes" of the car. *Chidi bitoo* is the term for gasoline and *bitoo* also means "stew" or "soup." Mutton stew is a staple of the Navajo diet and the connotations carry over to the way one's car is viewed. These and other terms are used in referring to an actual person—the syntax doesn't change. For instance, one could say "Sarah *bikee*" meaning "Sarah's feet or shoes" and "*chidi bikee*" meaning the tires on a car. The people have adapted the vocabulary to reflect the basic philosophy of Navajo life.

It would be easy to dismiss the environment of these photographs as desolate, barren, and isolated. Yet, for an Indian person, the land is rich with memories, stories, and sacred songs that ensure survival in this country. The huge rocks in Utah, near Kayenta, Shiprock pinnacle, and various others are strong places and exist for spiritual purposes. The desert is vast and expansive yet full of a power and a strength that few can comprehend.

Mr. Mitchell's stories show that the landscape and the people have an intricate connection that the human eye cannot perceive or the camera lens convey. The creation of various places are part of the framework of spirituality and world view that Navajo perceive life through. Seeing life as *hozhojii*—beauty and things being right and proper—is a constant attempt to balance the physical, mental, and spiritual at all times. *Hozhojii* does not exclude humor, irony or sadness. It involves family, school, work, and all aspects of ordinary life.

While it is a fact that the Navajo Nation is economically disadvantaged, thousands of Navajos have a clear understanding of what clans they belong to—therefore, the exact area or animal they originate from, who their relatives are, the responsibilities they have to others and to the land, and a strong sense of identity that many non-Indians cannot fathom.

It is with this in mind then, that these photographs should be viewed. The photographs document a people in transition, a culture in change, and yet cannot document the deep rootedness in history, the strong ties of language and songs, or the enduring hope in the eyes of the people. Those invisible facets are part of the way it was centuries ago, the way it will be, and the way it is now.

PHOTOGRAPHER'S NOTE

MIKE MITCHELL is a Navajo medicine person. The eleven stories were told in response to the pictures they face. They were spoken in Navajo, tape-recorded, transcribed, and translated verbatim. These transcripts then became the basis for a "translation." It was important to me to preserve the essence and meter of the stories as they were spoken. Storytelling is such a central tradition in Navajo culture that to polish them more would make them reflect the white culture and our ideas about storytelling more than the Navajo tradition as passed on by Mike.

It should also be noted that "picturetaking" is generally forbidden in Native American communities. The White Mountain Apache and Navajo nations that are represented by the majority of pictures in *Sign Language* are generally more accepting of the presence of cameras, except during ceremonies and when portraits are involved. The pictures were made with permission and exchange. Books and prints were given to each of those who posed, while the author's royalties are being donated to the Navajo Community College Press, in Tsaile, Arizona, toward future publication of Native American authors.

Taos Pueblo, New Mexico, 1983

Buffalo along Interstate 70 near Golden, Colorado, 1982

Curio trader's tee-pees near Meteor Crater, Arizona, 1982

Naaziigo naazh ch'aa

THEY SAY that some Ancient People (*Anaasazi*) made these rock piles and marks. Stories from somewhere long ago also say that not only the Ancient People made these rock piles. Below the rock piles made by the Ancient People are other rocks and rock caves.

It is said that there used to be dangerous beings, things in rock caves near this place vacated by the Ancient People. There used to be, among other things, wolf beings, and big tiger beings here. Hardly anyone went near the piles of rocks or caves, because big snakes used to live there long ago.

I have been told that the rock piles were also piled up by another group of people called the Bird People, who later somehow turned into human beings. Bird People are actually spirits personified who became human beings.

The Bird People lived in the caves and made their marks on rock piles. They were a clan of the Ancient People. If you study and look at their rock piles you can see that they are different from others. The difference is the fact that some are big rocks and some are small. They say the Bird People's rock piles are found at the bottom of other rock piles and in caves.

Someone said that the reason the Bird People piled rocks and made their homes in caves was because they were in danger. At that time when the Bird People would go hunting, they would sleep way up high in pine trees (halfway up or higher) on sticks that formed bridge-like platforms.

Two or three at a time went hunting, and they hunted for anything. The rock painted as a goat was one thing they hunted for. Next to the goat is a painted rock called *Naaziigo naazh ch'aa* (Pictured Standing), which was painted for protection. The white splashes (handprints) prove the existence of the Ancient People. The handprints really mean that they existed many years ago and painted the picture standing up. This is how the story was told.

Later others wrote on the rocks like this. There are rock piles made by earth people named Navajo. Today the Navajo are called the *Dine*, Holy People, while the rock piles of the Ancient People are a reference to the time before our Holy People emerged to this earth. Even though they say all of these writings on the rocks were done by the Ancient People, they are not all done by them.

—M. M.

Pictograph and tourist, Betatakin ruin, Navajo National Monument, Arizona, 1983

Navajo girls, archery competition, near Deer Springs, Arizona, 1986

Apache Gahn Spirit Dancers at Sunrise Ceremony, White River, Arizona, 1984

Apache drummer after Sunrise Ceremony, White River, Arizona, 1985

Navajo microwave transmission station near Goulding, Utah, 1984

Apache trickster posing with video camera used to record Sunrise Ceremony, White River, Arizona, 1985

Navajo housing project, Chinle, Arizona, 1984

THE PICTURE is of *Dook'o'oosliid* (San Francisco Peaks). They say the land there was repurchased. For this reason a ceremony was done and prayers were made. We are Navajo and Navajoland is our land's name.

Upland, the San Francisco Mountain Holy Being, spirit personified, sits. It contains prayers, it contains songs. It retains prayers, and it retains songs. They say that since prayers are contained there it was made holy. San Francisco is one of four Navajo Sacred Mountains.

San Francisco Peaks were made many millions of years ago to hold stories. Plans of life were placed there. Good minds and good thoughts were put there. Also, it has vegetation, food, eagles, four-legged animals, and birds. There are medicinal herbs on San Francisco Peaks. Also sacred stones are placed there. It holds everything. So it is right.

There are characteristics of its body which coexist with other living things. Specifically, animals, spirits personified, sheep, spirits personified, and human beings, spirits personified. The mountain was made for the purpose of spiritually coexisting with the material characteristics of the human race.

Many millions of years ago, when the Navajo were still carrying their own packs and hunting on foot, prayers and sacred stones were placed on top of the mountain. Rain and a good life were asked for future generations from that day forward. The San Francisco Mountain was made for this purpose.

Navajo people and all American Indians were given the mountain to protect the small and large game for food. The mountain was made in a holy way, exists in a holy way, and was placed on a sacred site. So it is that whatever lies on San Francisco, or is contained by it, belongs to the Navajo. All mountains everywhere are made holy with sacred characteristics.

In the future, we may live on the mountain without disturbing its spirit, and in the days to come, we may speak of the protection of its spirit.

In a similar way, we speak of these policemen representing the spirit of protection of things large and small. The policemen are standing with their horses in this way to speak or represent the spirit of spoken and written laws. The flags they are holding represent the spirit of the laws and constitution with which the American Indian lives. This is the way it is.

The Navajo human spirit really exists to speak the spiritual beliefs, its laws and minds. The policemen sit on their horses to protect the spiritual plans for the future.

The mountain, spirit personified, makes its plans no matter what lies upon it, new cars, a hogan, all the other earthly things. They say that is the way it will be.

So this is the way the mountain was formed. Its spirit was formed and later its purpose was recorded in nature.

May it be that as life expands and birth continues, our mountain is holy and plans for a good life and good mind are placed there. This is the reason it was made and placed there.

This is all I will tell.   —M. M.

Navajo Tribal Police presenting colors at celebration of lease-purchase of Sacred Mountain land, San Francisco Peaks, Arizona 1986

Fallout shelter directions near Goulding, Utah, 1984

Navajo medicine men discuss tribal government's lease-purchase of Sacred Mountain land, Rough Rock, Arizona, 1986

Apache tract housing near White River, Arizona, 1984

Navajo cinema and hogan, Tuba City, Arizona, 1985

Hooghan bika

THIS STORY is about the way a hogan is. Way back, who knows how many millions of years ago, the *Dine* (Navajo earth people) were put here to live and grow.

Certain land, including what is today called the Navajo Reservation, was chosen as Navajo land. The ancestors of the *Dine* were holy people. The *Dine* were holy beings when they were placed here. They were placed here with the hogan as their home.

A fire was lit inside the hogan. Everything from this fire outward to the mountains and vegetation was a part of the Navajo dwelling.

The hogan began with a door facing east and a hole at the top. It was placed so that its spirit breathed towards the east where the sun comes up in the morning. The sun shines through the doorway in the morning, and in midday it shines through the top hole. In a holy way the sun shines on it daily.

They say the hogan represents the mind. Life, love, and plans for the future are all dwellers in the hogan.

When it was created, the hogan was created as a mother. For this reason, the needs and plans for the future of those that dwell there will not be turned down.

From the hogan the Navajos talk, pray, and sing their respect for the mountains, canyons, streams, plants, animals, and everything else that exists.

The hogan has songs and prayers. For a happy dwelling, corn pollen from white corn is placed on the main poles and around the inside in a clockwise direction. When the main poles were set, it was turned into a Navajo spirit with its hands clutched to the ground.

This is the way it is and this is all I will tell about the hogan.

—M. M.

Navajo hogan, near Goulding, Utah, 1985

Spanish church ruin on ancient pueblo site, Pecos National Monument, New Mexico, 1983

Apache mother and child at weekend camp for Sunrise Ceremony, White River, Arizona, 1985

Men's room tiles, Hohokam Pima National Monument, Arizona, 1983

Hogan-shaped Administration Building, Navajo Community College, Tsaile, Arizona, 1984

Tacheeh

I N T H I S picture Apaches are taking sweat baths in a sweat house. All tribes of Indians have sweat houses. The reason for having sweat houses is for body refreshment so people can be lively and feel good. The Navajo word for sweathouse is *tacheeh*.

Sometimes people might feel lazy or tired, and they will put hot stones, as hot as they can stand, in the sweat house they are sitting in. Every now and then they come out and go in again. They quit when they think or feel their body has had enough heat, when they really feel good again.

That's one way a sweat house is used. Another time to use a sweat house is when a person is sick. There might be several kinds of sickness. The person might have aches and pains all over the body. Then a sweat house is used.

When the sweat house is being readied for a person who is sick, different kinds of herbal medicines are used, either boiled or natural. The sick person drinks some and some is laid on the floor of the sweat house. The sick body is brought in and taken care of that way.

Then there is the medicine person, who will also take care of sick people by praying and performing ceremonies with songs. Then the sick person gets well. This is another purpose for the sweat house.

When a person is very sick and has been given all kinds of help, and still is sick, even though it might seem useless, it is decided to have a sweat house ceremony with different types of herbal medicine. The herbal medicines will be drunk, while some will be put on the body and the floor of the sweat house. Medicine people perform ceremonies for others, and they perform ceremonies on themselves. From inside the sweat house they pray and sing songs in just the way of their beliefs. Regardless of how the patient is, if he or she does what the medicine person tells them to do, before you know it they are well.

The Navajos have sweat houses. Men have theirs and women have theirs. Like I said, the reason is for a good lively feeling—a good body, with good mind, and good plans. Whenever you feel you need it, take a sweat bath. These are the reasons different tribes of Indians all have sweat houses.

So this is the way the sweat house ceremony works, in many different ways in just the way it was given, way back, very strongly with herbal medicines in the veins throughout the body. Fire, rocks, water, and herbal medicine are set and working together in the sweat houses. It really works and gets people well again. This is why they just don't forget and walk off and leave their sweat houses. All the tribes of Indians hang on to their sweat houses. Who knows how long in the future it will exist?

This is the way I will end the story.

—M. M.

Apache Sweatlodge Ceremony, White River, Arizona, 1985

Kin-Li-Chee (Navajo) Tribal Park, Arizona, 1986

Zuni Lake, New Mexico, 1984

Navajo July 4 Pow Wow, Window Rock, Arizona, 1984

Navajo Monument Valley Tribal School near Goulding, Utah, 1985

Tse ghahoodzaani

THIS Window Rock place, *Tse ghahoodzaani,* contains a story about rocks. They tell stories about Window Rock long ago.

The hole of Window Rock used to contain prayers that would bring one back to reality. And, through prayers, some really bad things exited through the hole. They say, though, that one should never pass through the hole in Window Rock. This should never be done because once one passes through, there is no return.

Inside the rock and the hole in the rock there are things or spirits one should be aware of. For instance, when the wind is whirling through there, it will not return in the same direction it came through, and so one cannot be sure which way it will whirl, and which way some things will exit.

This hole in the rock called Window Rock is where the Navajo Tribal Government Headquarters are located. The plans for the livelihood of the tribe are made under Window Rock.

Long ago it was said that no prayer or ceremony should be done from the bottom of rocks because something might go wrong. The reason for this is that the rocks are not alive and cannot be moved. They represent stable, unmoving forces in nature.

But rocks are used in many different ways. From rocks we acquire our mind and thoughts, plans, life, silver, gold, and many more things.

Ceremonies are done with rocks. Whoever wanted to be a medicine person used to pray and place sacred stones beside them. These prayers and sacred stones were placed at a big rock, one that has rolled out on a plain when no others are around, a talking (echoing) rock, and whoever wants to be a medicine person can bless him or herself by rubbing on the rock. The rock does not move, so in the dark of night or even several nights the medicine person can sit/stand with the power to sit/stand strong. They say this was done that way.

In case you get hurt by a rock, then sacred stones should be placed next to it in order to use the rock. Rocks can also be used in a sweat house to heal you when you are sick.

If you arrive at the foot of a rock while traveling, you pick up a charcoal and draw a cross on it before retiring for the night. The cross should be drawn upward first then left to right.

They say that when rocks were created, they were formed into a rock man, rock woman, rock boy and rock girl (Holy Spirits). The rocks are talked and prayed to in this respect, and corn pollen is placed on them.

I will end the story on the rock here.

—M. M.

Biker at Navajo tribal government grounds, Window Rock, Arizona, 1984

San Carlos Apache housing development, Arizona, 1984

Strip mining on Navajo land near Shiprock, New Mexico, 1986

Dzilyigiin

Coal is being mined. The earth is being broken up, and coal is taken out. Several places are being mined this way. Uranium, coal, and many others that are inside of Mother Earth are mined and taken out and placed on the body of the earth.

Years back, elderly ladies and men had stories about our Mother Earth. Our Mother Earth was made with life. Whatever Mother Earth was made with was put here to make our living with, that's the way they told the story.

Whatever is brought up to the surface from the inside is for our use. That is what they mean by Mother Earth, which was made in harmony with living things. Earthly Five-Fingered People (human beings) must somehow be able to make a living.

Whatever the Five-Fingered People got from the surface and whatever they picked that was grown on it will be respectful of their loving relationship with Mother Earth, they said.

For this reason Mother Earth shared her property with the Navajo people to live within the four sacred mountains.

Then the Holy People, the First Lady, the First Man, and Changing Woman existed. *Hashcheltii'i* and *Hashch'eyaan* and many other Holy People existed. They are the ones who said our Navajo children will be here, and here they will live in the future. Our children will make a livelihood and multiply here. The Holy People put the livelihood or subsistence in and on Mother Earth for us to live a full life.

In the future, who knows in how many millions of years, we will destroy everything when we use up everything. We will have sucked everything out from Mother Earth with nothing left. This will happen if we don't take care of Mother Earth. That will be the end they say.

They say the end will really happen when our prayers, songs, and our livelihood are forgotten. Our Mother Earth will be bare of everything with nothing more to take. At that time, it would be called the end of the world. Whoever or whatever is doing this to us (our enemies whom we cannot see) will put an end to our livelihood.

For that reason, even though it is our Mother Earth being dug out, we say be careful, don't take too much or our unity will be broken down. Yet it is still being done on account of the expanding generation. It does not slow down. The Navajo people try to make use of whatever we can get to support ourselves. We try to save so we can eat to feel good to go on again.

Probably, this is what our past grandfathers and grandmothers meant. They foresaw what was coming to the future generation's livelihood. This mining coal, uranium, oil, gas, and whatever else for our livelihood is using everything. For that reason we must keep and think of it as a holy place.

This is the way they told it, so for that reason we should carefully keep it holy by our ceremonies, prayers, and songs. That is the only way our carelessness will slow down.

This is as far as I will tell of the story. This is it.

—M. M.

Navajo men measuring drill holes for blasting at Black Mesa Coal Mine, Arizona, 1986

Natural gas refinery on Navajo land near Leupp, Arizona, 1986

Navajo Power Plant and Shiprock, New Mexico, 1986

Apache strip mining and reclamation near McNary, Arizona, 1984

Navajo boys shooting bottles near Tuba City, Arizona, 1984

Bit'siis nineezi

Wʜᴀᴛ ʏᴏᴜ see is irrigation water on a plain. Water is flowing. Long ago water was made and put on the earth in a holy way.

Water is really used in many ways. It is also used in ceremonies, in a holy way. There are holy songs and prayers for it.

Water flows endlessly when you see it, and its names are *Bit'siis nineezi* (long body) and *Bits'iis binakaa yec tii* (see through body). When you look at it from here you just see water flowing.

Specifically, all growing and living things, and plants of all kinds live to stay wet, breathe, and grow with water. So water has its purpose. Plants, and growing and moving animals, including human beings, and other living things live on it. It's their main juice, their body, their heart, their blood veins, and their minds. Put all together, it is their whole being. It is the root of life, like a good mind to plan a good livelihood, such as a good life with love.

Where water is, there are living things. Where water is, life goes on. In a holy way it flows. It is alive in a holy way. So they say it is very holy. Water is our main source of life. Doctors all use water. Believers of all denominations always use water.

For that reason, many generations back the Navajos used to keep it sacred in many different ways (as is true in the present and the future). It is used in ceremonies. You pray with it when you drink water, and put water on yourself when praying.

There are oceans around the world. There is water inside and outside the earth, even up in the sky where mist and frost form. So precious is water that we have a great love and respect for our living water.

When you don't feel good you drink water by itself, it will take care of all ailments in your body's systems. Drink water and pray, and it will take care of all your ailments. Sprinkle water around, sit, pray, and drink, and you'll feel better.

When the plants and everything begin to dry up, a ceremony will take place that could prepare for the rain. The old people say this ceremony was handed down from generation to generation. Prayers, songs, corn pollen, and sacred stones are placed at water streams. Between the first and the fourth day, it starts to rain. They say the water listens and hears prayers and songs with sacred stones. When this takes place, the rewards are great and holy. Clouds start to gather, followed by rain, and everything gets back to life.

All of a sudden rain starts pouring down out of the sky, and it really rains. Everywhere there is water.

Where and how water was made, nobody knows. When water was put on Mother Earth it was made so it will never cease. Nobody knows how many millions of years ago it was made. To this day it still exists. Even though people have many uses for it such as irrigation, water will never cease.

Pray to it, talk to it, respect it, and keep it holy. That's what will save it for future use. Take care of it with ceremony, even if it's just small drops of water. Pray for a good life leading into old age.

Ask water to give you prayers, ask water to help you make plans, and for a good life so you can walk in beauty. This was the prayer in the former days, as in the present and the future.

This is the way the Navajo people tell the story about water.

—ᴍ.ᴍ.

Navajo Irrigation Project near Shiprock, New Mexico, 1986

Apache women grading lumber at tribal mill, White River, Arizona, 1985

Road cut through mesa on Navajo land near Chichinbito, Arizona, 1987

Navajo jewelry sales, Elephant Feet, Arizona, 1984

Apache home and business, White River, Arizona, 1984

Atl'o

THIS IS a hogan setting from the inside. A rug loom is up. There is a Navajo lady called Navajo Mother and maybe a granddaughter sitting with her.

This is the way the hogan is.

They say the mind and life's plans lie in the inside of the hogan setting. They say life lies inside, hope is inside, love lies inside. All of which the hogan was made with, they say.

They say this is why there is a fire burning in the middle of the hogan. This is why today there lies a fire in the middle of the hogan burning in a stove.

Hogans hold everything from there, earthly things of all kinds, sacred stones of all kinds. They say that what they contain, whatever they hold, is called First Hand because this is where a livelihood is planned. This is told that way. They say it holds whatever stories it contains.

A grinding stone for food, a rock brush, stirring sticks, beat-up-and-down sticks, and tools for rug-making are lying there. That is what it is made of and living a good life is its purpose.

The hogan was made with the spirits of prayers and songs inside. This affects the minds and plans of those who live there. In the doorway to the east, there is a man and woman together. They live together with the little children there.

The rug loom and rugs really have a lot of stories with them. A lot of good thoughts are acting with the different designs and colors. The art pattern in the rug is formed by the mind inside, the mind acting in the body. They say the pattern-forming takes place first in the mind, then it forms within the rug. That is the way the mind works plans out in the rug.

This is the way the hogan is made up, so this is the size of it.

—M. M.

Interior of Navajo weaver's hogan, Monument Valley Tribal Park, Arizona, 1985

Navajo pre-med student, Navajo Community College, Tsaile, Arizona, 1986

Gasoline pump, Navajo Monument Valley Tribal School near Goulding, Utah, 1986

Apache woman, White River, Arizona, 1984

San Carlos Apache recreation center near San Carlos, Arizona, 1984

Entering Hopi land from Navajo land, Arizona, 1985

Apache butcher, White River, Arizona, 1984

"As the Mementoes of the Race"

PHOTOGRAPHS OF NORTH AMERICAN INDIANS

BY MARTHA A. SANDWEISS

IN MID-1845, while on a lecture tour in Great Britain, the Reverend Peter Jones was photographed by the great Scottish photographers Hill and Adamson. He posed several times in his clerical garb. But his skill as a religious orator was not his main attraction for the photographers. Jones, the son of a Welsh surveyor and an Ojibway Indian woman, had been raised as an Ojibway until his father removed him from the tribe at the age of sixteen. Now a Methodist and a bilingual missionary to his mother's tribe, he represented to the Europeans an exotic American world. So Hill and Adamson also photographed him in traditional dress, with a feather-decorated hat on his head and a tomahawk in his hand. This photograph of Jones, known also as Kahkewaquonaby, is recognized as the earliest photograph of a North American Indian.

It seems ironic that this first picture of the most American of types should have been made so far from home, yet the image is oddly prophetic of the thousands of photographs of Indians that would be made in the succeeding decades. Kahkewaquonaby is presented in a formal and serious pose, as an exotic type removed from his own environment and arranged by the photographer in an alien world. The portrait of this highly educated and well-traveled man in traditional clothing belies the reality of his personal experience and the culture of his mother's people who had long had contact with white explorers and Euro-American trade goods. Thus the image has a retrospective quality that reflects the photographers' effort to create an image of "authentic," unadulterated Indian culture that ignores the realities of historical change. This romantic desire to fix for posterity the image of a distant past or an imagined present would prove the distinguishing characteristic of most nineteenth- and early twentieth-century photographs of American Indians.

The first photographs of American Indians made in the United States are probably those of Thomas Easterly, whose daguerreotypes of Keokuk, a renowned Sauk and Fox chief, were made near Liberty, Missouri in 1846 or 1847. When Easterly moved to St. Louis in 1848 he advertised a curious assortment of daguerreotypes including "likenesses of Distinguished Statesmen, Eminent Divines, Prominent Citizens, Indian Chiefs, and Notorious Robbers and Murderers." His Indian subjects pose in their own clothing but sitting in a photographic studio they, like most other subjects of the daguerrian's art, seem sadly divorced from their own environment and the material accoutrements of their life.[1]

It is not known what either Kahkewaquonaby or Keokuk thought of their pictures, but scattered accounts suggest that an individual Indian's response to the camera was conditioned by both traditional beliefs and previous experiences with Euro-American culture. There is a widely-held belief that Indians regarded the camera as a device that could steal their very souls. But it is hard to corroborate this idea through contemporary sources. As with so many other popular beliefs about nineteenth-century Indians, it is at best a gross racial generalization that gives little regard to the widely varied beliefs and experiences of different peoples. John Mix Stanley, photographing the Blackfeet at Fort Benton on the upper Missouri River in 1853, was warmly received by his subjects who were "delighted and astonished to see their likenesses produced by direct action of the sun. They worship the sun, and they consider Mr. Stanley was inspired by their divinity, and he thus became in their eyes a great medicine man." Similarly, Solomon Carvalho found that the Cheyennes he encountered in his trip across Kansas in 1853 "worshipped me as possessing extraordinary powers of necromancy." But Carl Wimar, who tried to photograph the Mandan in 1858, was rebuffed by people who, recalling the smallpox epidemic introduced by previous white visitors, feared that the photographer and his camera would reintroduce the disease.[2]

Just as it is inappropriate to assume a monolithic "Indian" attitude toward photography, so it would be wrong to assume that all Native Americans in the nineteenth century had the same attitude toward photographers. Nonetheless, it seems fair to surmise that photographers working in the field were generally perceived as agents of another society whose interests were at odds with those of the native cultures. Hence the unwitting significance of J. Wesley Jones's story of an encounter with unspecified Indians at a site called Steeple Rocks in 1852. Jones, intent upon an ambitious project to daguerreotype the entire overland route to the California gold fields, had stopped to photograph a rock formation when suddenly he found himself surrounded by "a war party of Indians." He aimed his camera at the "savages," began firing his revolver from beneath his darkcloth, and held a lighted cigar in proximity to his apparatus. According to Jones, the Indians, who had heard "strange stories of thunder on wheels which had, in one terrific burst, swept away whole

parties of red skin," fled in fear of the camera/cannon.[3] The camera may not have been a true instrument of violence, but it was an agent of the social and political forces that were forcing violent change upon the Indian peoples as the line of Euro-American settlement moved westward across the plains.

Thus it seems inevitable that some early photographers should find themselves caught up in violence precipitated as much by their very presence as by their particular line of work. Sioux Indians in Idaho Territory destroyed the photographic equipment of a Mr. and Mrs. Larimer in 1864 and, after injuring Mr. Larimer, took his wife captive. Photographer Ridgway Glover, a correspondent for the *Philadelphia Photographer,* was killed by Sioux Indians in Montana Territory in September, 1866. Sergeant Wylyams, an assistant to the British-born photographer Dr. William Bell, who had been engaged in 1867–68 to make views along a proposed southern route for a transcontinental railroad, was killed in violence at Fort Wallace. The bloodshed, of course, was caused by whites as well. Countless Indians were killed by the soldiers in the military units these photographers accompanied through the West. Deeply ingrained cultural assumptions and territorial needs on both sides made such violence inevitable.[4]

Whether they worked in a controlled studio setting or in the field, nineteenth-century photographers had ample opportunity to arrange their Indian subjects and manipulate their surroundings. In the Washington D.C. studios where members of visiting Indian delegations were systematically photographed for anthropological purposes from 1858 on, sitters were generally posed on elaborately patterned carpets or "rusticated" floors covered with fake grass, tree stumps, and carefully fabricated rocks. Draped tables, upholstered chairs, trompe-l'oeil backdrops, and other typical Victorian studio props often appear beside the traditionally garbed sitters. Studio locations in the West, at military forts or in border towns near Indian settlements, did not necessarily provide more authentic settings. Working at Fort Sill, Indian Territory from 1870 to 1874, for instance, Maine-born photographer Will Soule made portraits of Indian subjects posed in front of a painted backdrop that better suggested a pastoral New England lake than a scene on the Great Plains. It would be difficult, however, to imagine a more ridiculous setting than that contrived by G. W. Parsons, a photographer working in Pawhuska, Oklahoma Territory in the 1890s. In his studio, Parsons photographed Indian subjects in front of a lavishly painted backdrop, using as props an Egyptian-revival settee, an imitation wrought iron gate, and a floor decorated with pieces of straw and grass and cats-o'-nine-tails carefully glued to stand stiffly upright.

Photographers working outdoors generally included more of their Indian subjects' own environment, but even these photographers sometimes manipulated a sitter's appearance to reflect their own imagined notions of Indian life. In 1873 John K. Hillers, who served as photographer for Major John Wesley Powell's Colorado River surveys of the early 1870s, worked with the painter Thomas Moran, whose job was to arrange the photographer's Indian subjects in artful poses. These two transformed traditional women into seductive temptresses with looks and poses borrowed from the conventions of European painting. Hiller's subjects generally wore their own, if carefully arranged, clothing. But on one occasion Hillers photographed a Paiute woman wearing a White River Ute dress collected on a previous government expedition and carried back to the field by Powell. Close examination of the picture reveals its absurdity: a Smithsonian Institute catalogue number is emblazoned across the woman's bodice. The camera might have been an objective recording instrument, but the cameraman was not. Or, as the twentieth-century documentary photographer Lewis Hine once wrote, "While photographs may not lie, liars may photograph."[5]

Most photographers of Indians during the nineteenth century were imbued with a sense of historic purpose. Agents of change themselves, they nonetheless wanted to fix for posterity a visual record of a seemingly dying race. Promoting his portraits of Indian delegates to the nation's capital, Washington, D.C. photographer James McClees wrote in the late 1850s, "To the student of our history, as additions to libraries and historical collections, and as the momentoes of the race of red men, now rapidly fading away, this series is of great value and interest." In 1877, geologist Ferdinand V. Hayden oversaw the production of a catalogue listing over a thousand photographs gathered together by the United States Geological and Geographical Survey. Part of the purpose of the collection, he wrote, was to provide physical information to anthropologists then engaged in the fashionable practice of studying head measurements of the different races. But its greatest value was as a historical record. "Now that the tribal relations of these Indians are fast being successively sundered by the process of removal to reservations, which so greatly modifies the habits and particularly the style of dress of the aborigines, the value of such a graphic record of the past increases year by year; and there will be no more trustworthy evidence of what the Indians have been than that afforded by these faithful sun-pictures. . . ."[6]

Looking back, it sometimes seems as if every photographer thought he or she would be the last to capture a truly authentic picture of traditional Indian life. Nearly half a century after McClees boasted that *his* pictures captured a life that was almost gone, Edward Curtis wrote in the introduction to his monumental forty-volume work *The North American Indian* (1907–1930) that *he* had just barely caught a true image of Indian life. "The great changes in practically every phase of the Indian's life that have taken place, especially within recent years, have been such that had the time for collecting much of the material . . . been delayed, it would have been lost forever." Two decades later, in 1926, Laura Gilpin justified her photographs of a play about ancient southwestern Indian life by writing, "the life, the customs, the very types which the play represents are passing away with a speed that frightens one. Quite aside from my photographer's interest in its scenes, I am eager to add one more bit of accurate pictorial information about these Indians to the pitifully small amount we possess."[7]

For photographers intent upon creating a historical record, it was but a small step to deliberately fabricate one. And by the turn of the century, as the reality of white-Indian warfare receded into memory and tribes were confined to reservations, it became easier to view the Indian past through the gauze of romantic sentiment. Rapid changes may have been taking place in traditional life, but that is not what photographers wanted to see. Relying on omission and a highly selective camera vision, they created an illusive record of Indian life. Walter McClintock, who first went west with a forestry expedition in 1896 shortly after his graduation from Yale, photographed the Blackfoot Indians of northern Montana for several years, without ever suggesting the presence or influence of the nearby town of Browning. Gertrude Käsebier created sensitive, highly romantic Indian portraits in her New York studio in 1898 that never betray the fact that her subjects were performers in Buffalo Bill's Wild West Show. When Laura Gilpin photographed at Laguna Pueblo in 1924 she waited several hours in order to make a view of the church that would not include automobiles. When she went to Zuni Pueblo on this same trip and could not find a girl to pose in traditional white leggings, she simply photographed her subject from the knees up. The prevailing pictorial aesthetic of early twentieth-century photography which valued a hazy, soft-focus style of printing was well suited to popular attitudes of the time, characterized by an equally romantic and hazy view of Indian life. For writers and political reformers as well as photographers, it was common to view Native Americans as unindividuated, romanticized types.

Thus anthropologists and historians who work with nineteenth- and early twentieth-century photographs of American Indians must be wary of the pictures' true informational value. To accept the photograph as a statement of "fact" without examining the photographer's motivations and the circumstances under which the picture was made is as unsound a practice as accepting the truth of a diary without considering its author. Indeed, the pictures may reveal more about their maker than their subject; they may tell more about the prevailing values of the photographer's culture than they do about the culture they purport to document.

During the 1930s, a new emphasis on documentary photography emerged in this country as government agencies—in particular the Farm Security Administration—put photographers to work recording depression-era America. But American Indians, many living on reservations far-removed from the focus of New Deal economic programs, went undocumented by this army of photographers. Only a few independent workers saw on the reservations a problem worthy of the attention of economic and social reformers. And they, giving broader attention to the actual circumstances of reservation life, helped develop the more straightforward and inclusive style of photodocumentary that has characterized most contemporary efforts by white outsiders to record Indian life.

Working in collaboration with the writer-reformer Oliver La Farge, photographer Helen M. Post created a photodocument of tribal life from the northern plains to the southwest pueblos. Published in *As Long As the Grass Shall Grow: Indians Today* (1940), her pictures reveal the enormous cultural and economic problems incurred by federal government policies and misguided do-gooders and, at the same time, suggest the great economic potential of self-governing Indian groups. Her pictures are about a lively present, full of contradictions and a problematic mixture of traditional practices and imported conveniences.

Gilpin, turned down for a job with the Farm Security Administration because her work seemed too sentimental, became increasingly unsentimental and more documentary as she photographed the Navajo people in the early 1930s, then on through the 1950s and '60s. Concerned in the beginning with creating a photographic record that documented the "old ways," she eventually became more interested in recording a more inclusive view of Navajo life that examined how the old and new ways could coexist in a rapidly evolving culture: how industry could benefit the tribe, how self-government could function, how highly educated students could retain their ties to Navajo traditionalism and find employment back on the reservation. Like Post, she conceived of her pictures as both works of art and social documents. Allying her images with a text of her own in *The Enduring Navaho* (1968), she set forth her own concerns about the future of the Navajo people.

Gilpin and Post both gave great moral weight to Indian traditionalism. Yet, with their straightforward acknowledgment of the changing social and economic conditions of reservation life, they provide a kind of bridge between the romantic, backward-looking photographs of their nineteenth- and early twentieth-century predecessors and the pictures of Skeet McAuley, who is among the relatively few white photographers to continue working within this long tradition. Since the Indian rights movement of the 1960s and the emergence of a new generation of Native American artists, photographers, and politicians, few outsiders like McAuley have ventured to make extended photographic documents of native communities. Indian photographers, such as Hopi artist Victor Masayesva, Jr., have emerged as the chroniclers of their own people.

Photographs made by Indians are, of course, not necessarily different from those made by anyone else. The overwhelming number of photographs made by Indians, like those made by any ethnic or cultural

IAIA SWdwh

group in America, are family snapshots. Indian students are probably as subject to the vagaries and trends of contemporary photographic fashion as their non-Indian classmates. But those who, like Masayesva, use photography as a means of documenting their own culture have a vantage point and perspective denied all outsiders. And yet, this increased access does not automatically translate into a more comprehensive photographic document. If a general purpose of the outside photographer is to reveal information about a native group, one intent of the native photographer may be to conceal it. Certain tribal traditions must be preserved and protected. "Even if you are a Hopi photographing a Hopi," Masayesva writes, "you will not confront the silences." Refraining from photographing certain subjects, he says, becomes a kind of worship.[8]

The inheritor of a long tradition of picture-making by outsiders in Indian communities, McAuley nonetheless alters the conventions of this tradition in important ways. By using humor and irony in his photographs he eschews the tradition of high seriousness with which most of his predecessors worked. While most nineteenth-century photographers, impelled by a keen sense of their own higher mission, made solemn portraits of their seemingly noble subjects, McAuley has no such notions of self-importance. Though he works with a view camera as did most of his predecessors and thus cannot make spontaneous snapshots, he nonetheless manages to make pictures that are humorous, several of which stand out: the window washer at Monument Valley cleaning glass as if a tourist couldn't just step outside and get an unimpeded view of the rock formations through the crystal clear desert air; the Indian children practicing with store-bought bows and arrows; the sprinkler trying to coax a green lawn from the sun-baked earth around Pecos National Monument. Sometimes, it is just the unexpected juxtaposition of things that seems funny, such as the beautifully tended grass on a desert football field or the space-age mural in a desert-bound school.

Like Post or Gilpin, who more than any nineteenth-century photographers set the stage for what he is trying to do, McAuley deliberately embraces both the old and the new in his photographs and routinely photographs his subjects in their own environments. But unlike these women, he adopts an apolitical stance and never purports to be a reformer. His pictures are not as much about cultural declension and loss,

as about cultural change and adaptation. And change, for him, is neither good nor bad; it is merely a fact. The new suburban-style house he photographs on a neatly curved street in front of miles of empty desert seems neither better nor worse than a traditional hogan. Instead, it seems ironic—ironic that a suburban landscape should be imposed on a land where space is readily available, where families have traditionally lived far from their neighbors, where different building materials more appropriate to the environment have already been developed.

Because he does not believe in an "authentic," culturally-pristine past from which his Indian subjects have fallen away, and has no political point to belabor, McAuley is free to photograph what he finds. He does not need to create scenes that suggest an imagined past or falsely-conceived present. The irony of what is there, right now, is what attracts him. And the color in McAuley's pictures accentuates the irony found in his deliberate juxtapositions of old and new, traditional and nontraditional. The green grass, yellow signs, and red gas pumps leap out at the viewer from the more muted palette of the desert southwest. This color adds a touch of realism to the scenes: it makes it impossible to view McAuley's subjects as pieces of a romantic and dimly-seen monochromatic past.

But I speak as a *bilagáana,* the Navajo word for a white person. The narratives in this book by Navajo medicine man Mike Mitchell offer a powerful reminder that photographic meaning is a highly subjective thing, and that the photographer can successfully impose meaning upon a scene only to the extent that the viewer shares the photographer's own cultural assumptions. I look at McAuley's pictures in one way; Mitchell looks at them in another. Where I see evidence of material change, Mitchell sees evidence of spiritual continuity. While I seize on the incongruity of the new, he focuses on the continuing force of the ancient. It is humbling for me to be reminded that what I see as funny or ironic or beautiful in these pictures is not necessarily funny or ironic or beautiful to any of the people who come out of the culture that the photographer depicts.

Ultimately, Mitchell's comments on these pictures are not only humbling, but reassuring as they reveal the limitations of photography as a tool of cultural explication. Most nineteenth-century photographers of

American Indians felt confident that they could capture the very essence of native history and culture on film. Mitchell's remarks show us just how wrong they were. Visual information does not give us spiritual knowledge. That remains a deeply private thing impervious to the all-seeing eye of the camera.

NOTES

1. John C. Ewers, "Thomas M. Easterly's Pioneer Daguerreotypes of Plains Indians," *Missouri Historical Society Bulletin* 24 (July, 1968): 331.

2. Robert Taft, *Photography and the American Scene: A Social History, 1839–1889* (1938, rpt. New York: Dover Publications Inc., 1964), pp. 262–63; Paula Richardson Fleming and Judith Luskey, *The North American Indians in Early Photographs* (New York: Harper & Row, 1986), p. 194.

3. J. Wesley Jones [with John Dix], *Amusing and Thrilling Adventures of a California Artist....* (Boston, published for the author, 1854), pp. 31–32.

4. Sarah L. Larimer, *The Capture and Escape; or Life Among the Sioux* (Philadelphia: Claxton, Remsem & Haffelfinger, 1870); Fanny Kelly, *Narrative of My Captivity among the Sioux Indians* (Cincinnati: Wilstach, Baldwin & Co., 1871), p. 38; William A. Bell, *New Tracks in North America* (London: Chapman and Hall, 1869), pp. 62–65.

5. Lewis Hine, "Social Photography: How the Camera May Help in the Social Uplift," *Proceedings of the National Conference of Charities and Corrections* (June, 1909), reprinted in Alan Trachtenberg, ed., *Classic Essays on Photography* (New Haven: Leete's Island Books, 1980), p. 111.

6. Fleming and Luskey, p. 22; William Henry Jackson, *Descriptive Catalogue of Photographs of North American Indians* (Washington, D.C.: Government Printing Office, 1877), p. iii.

7. Beth Barclay DeWall, "Edward Sheriff Curtis: A New Perspective on 'The North American Indian'," *History of Photography* 6 (July 1982): 223; Mildred Adams, "A Worker in Light," *Woman Citizen* 54 (March 1926): 11.

8. Victor Masayesva, Jr. and Erin Younger, *Hopi Photographers, Hopi Images* (Tucson: University of Arizona Press, 1983), p. 9.

ACKNOWLEDGMENTS

THIS PROJECT has not been one of autonomy. Over the past six years countless people have influenced the work and its "products" of book and exhibition. Acknowledgment of all would not only be impossible but also somehow incomplete. Some will inevitably be forgotten, and I apologize now. Commensurate thanks go to all.

In an inverted fashion, recognition goes first to some of those who unknowingly affected *Sign Language*: Edward Curtis, Adam Clark Vroman, Timothy O'Sullivan, Henry Jackson, Ansel Adams, Robert Adams, Lewis Baltz, Linda Connor, and Joel Sternfeld; John Ford, John Wayne, and the rest of Hollywood's representations of "Indians in the Wild West"; the "Western Art" community; the United States Government and its many agents: George Armstrong Custer, Kit Carson, William Sherman, and James Watt; and most of all those who have written words which shed real light on the subject of this book: Dee Brown, Vine Deloria, Jr., Leslie Silko, Jamake Highwater, Louise Erdrich, Lame Deer, Edward Abbey, and Tony Hillerman.

A physical hand has been lent by: all those who have allowed the camera into their homes, businesses, and ceremonies; Paolo Contu, Jerri Council, Navajo Community College Housing, Joan Myers/Gary Dewalt, Geanna Merola/Erik Landsburg, and the rest who have allowed me a place to stay, camp, and especially shower; David Begay, Vickie Morris, Mike Mitchell, Andy Natonabah, Ursula Wilson, and Faye Bia Knoki, who were instrumental to the recording, transcription, translation, and paraphrasing of the Navajo stories; Ray Smith, Joe Horner, Rex Jobe, and the others who put up with my perfectionism at The Color Place; Charlie Stainback, who got my foot in Aperture's door; Steve Dietz, who made a stand when it was most needed; Peter Andersen, who made it look good; and my wife, Lee Hutchins, who for the duration of the project has put up with "Skeet's trips," picking up the loose ends while I was away.

Two National Endowment for the Arts Individual Artist Fellowships came at critical times in the shooting and printing of this project. Navajo Community College in Tsaile, Arizona financed the Navajo stories. The Color Place of Dallas has done more than its fair share with its support of the printing, while the Ilford Corporation of Paramus, New Jersey has also lent a hand. The Amon Carter Museum of Fort Worth, Texas has not only morally supported the work from early on, but also taken on the giant task of exhibiting and traveling the prints nationally. The University of North Texas in Denton, Texas gave me valuable time when I needed it, while also funding some of the printing materials. Texas Books, Inc. of Dallas generously supported the publication, as did the Vaughn Foundation of Tyler, Texas, Lemuel C. and Martha Joe Hawes Hutchins, and a private donor who wished to remain anonymous.

Finally, a special appreciation goes to Scott Momaday, Luci Tapahonso, Mike Mitchell, and Marni Sandweiss for completing the intended cultural reciprocation with their essays and stories.

The staff at Aperture for *Sign Language* is Michael E. Hoffman, Executive Director;
Steve Dietz, Editor; Lisa Rosset, Managing Editor; Stevan Baron, Production Director;
Glynis Aiken, Tessa Lowinsky, Miranda Ottewell, and Jane D. Marsching, Editorial Work-Scholars.
Book design by Peter Andersen.

Aperture Foundation, Inc. publishes a periodical, books, and portfolios of fine
photography to communicate with creative people everywhere. A complete
catalog is available upon request. Address: 20 East 23 Street,
New York, New York, 10010.